Love
Spell

Love Spell

A Collection of Poetry Written

By

RAINY PAYNE

Copyright © 2016 In More Than Words
No part of this book may be reproduced in any form or by any electronic or mechanical means including information storage and retrieval systems without prior permission from the publisher in writing.

Cover design and illustration: Rainy Payne

Printed in the United States of America

ISBN: 978-0-578-17467-9

To my past, present, and future loves. Thank you for inspiring this poetry.

CONTENTS

	Page
The Search	3
Ex-Ray	5
Housaholic	9
When It Rains	11
Play	15
Erase	17
To My Song	21
The Waiting Game	23
Amnesia	27
L.O.V.E.	29
On A Day Like This	33
Clouds	35
Night Vision	37
Love Defined	41
Pen, Paper, Prose	43
Less Than	45
Connected	49

Flowers	51
Two Years	53
Behind Closed Doors	57
Psycho	59
Afraid	63
Your Eyes	65
Carry On	67
Unspoken	69
Free Spirit	71
The Means	73
What Am I?	75
Remember Me	79

"I pray thee, gentle mortal, sing again. Mine ear is much enamored of thy note. So is mine eye enthralled to thy shape. And thy fair virtue's force perforce doth move me on the first view to say, to swear, I love thee."

William Shakespeare
A Midnight Summer's Dream (3.7.137-41)

THE SEARCH

In search to find myself, I find you.
A love that will last past this lifetime.
Making your mark on my heart like a melody.
You are my favorite song.

And for so long I have wanted your lofty lyrical lilt
    of love to softly seduce me.
Easily overcome, I am yours a first glance.
First kiss.
By lips that never knew my name until now.

You are my reoccurring dream.
I have seen you there where you have held my
    hand and taught me how to fly.
By shedding light on the loveless life I've led
    before.
You've made all those years of being lost and alone
    worth the weary wait.
And only fate can take the blame for being between
    this blessing.

We were in waiting for the right time in space.
Searching to find.
Sorting out.
Simplifying self.
Trying to find what it feels like to be fearless.
Freeing ourselves of fault.

In the midst, I find my prince.

Perfect.

All my clues left in random **dé·jà vus** led me to find you.
Our hearts now harbor a harmony that only two can hear.
My remedy.
Reviving the romance that resides deep inside.
Dormant no longer.

Finally, I find you.

Finally, you find me.

EX RAY

On a night when daylight was saving its time.
My stomach was grumbling rumbling with the
    pangs of hunger.
So, I fought the rain and thunder to a trendy little
    spot for late night eats.
Glowing and unknowing I was being viewed on a
    higher level of a master plan.
Standing.
    Sitting.
        I took the menu from his hand.

Yeah, he is definitely a Jedi master with all those
    Jedi tricks.
Slick quick to the game was I at this first encounter;
    that I put my ante on the table and waited for
    this joker to deal.

"Is there anything else I can get you?" He asked.
As my mind wandered to something other than my
    meal.

He must have read my expression.
A confession of what I was thinking.
My blushing and blinking closed the deal.

I smiled, and he smiled back.

And it was more like telepathy between our stare.
Something more that spoken word could say.
The trap was set.
I was cornered, caught, and ambushed by my ex
   Ray.

In the beginning, things were better than they were
   in the end.
We would hang out and make out until I
   considered him more than just a friend.
Close were we.
Well, as close as he wanted me to be.
Until one night fright set in as I said to he,

"You are fire and I am water. When we touch, we
   make hot steam. Condensation the joins and
   flows with the sweat of our love. And it should
   be set free. For it is a beautiful song bird with a
   melody yet unheard."

"Word." He said.
With a calm composure.
A quiet anxiety of what my words revealed about
   my emotions.
My devotion.
Causing a commotion with his intention.
I was exactly where he wanted me to be.

He had me silly and dizzy with the kissin', but
   there was something I was definitely missin'.
Cause our love was just a dream.

LOVE SPELL

Seems since my confession, he threw away his
    possession.
He would speak to me like I was his favorite tease.
Not willing to repent and never willing to please.
And I translucent under magnified light, followed
    him painfully on my knees.
With the slightest stroke of his hands I was at his
    command.

Now, understand.
I was spellbound, bewitched by the voodoo he do.
And you would be too if you were me and I were
    you.
True to nothing I believed in before.
Setting myself up for an uneven score, a closed
    door.

You see.
I was strapped, trapped handicapped by his hands,
    his body, the way he smelled, and his voice.
Blindly making decisions, a compulsive choice.

To choose my wayward love's path all gone astray.
Before I knew what hit me, I was lost in love lust
    love with my ex Ray.

Pinched by his charms and stunned by his
    splendor.
My heart was in a blender.
But so tender was his game that when he was
    through with me I was left ashamed; with no

one but myself to blame.
What was strong was now weak.
Four months of fast forward took two years to untweak.
Reclaimed the few pieces of my heart and took back my dignity.
He played a major part in how I will let others treat me.

Now, to this day I can't say I don't have feelings for him still.
The thrill of our moments together.
Still looking deeper.
Still searching for something that was real.
I know one day our paths will cross and I don't know what I will do or say.
Leave him be?
Or have some steamy play, with my ex Ray?

HOUS-A-HOLIC

Hello. My name is Rainy and I am a house music
    junkie.
I've tried to be strong, but I can't pull off a pretend.
As the relapse begins my body gives in to the
    melodies that mesmerize.
Dipping deep in each riff of the reverberations that
    awaken the itch for more.
For, the sounds that seep into my skin.
Penetrating piercing my eardrum drumming
    strumming my captivated collective.
Mentally lapping a language that's beyond linear
    linguistics.
Taking in all I can take, I assimilate the visual
    verbiage that's shaking my mind body soul.

I am a
        house
                music
                      junkie.

Taking no time to tease this seduction coyly
    consumes my consciousness.
Taking control.
I am a house head with a habit.
I don't hesitate to indulge in a hit of high-frequency
    sounds soaking me.
Making me slippery.

Settling my cerebral synapses.
Quenching my mental melodic thirst.
Getting drunk, I drink in every delicious drop.
I lick the kick from the drums that draw me like a
 moth to a flickering flame.
Tame is not the word to explain my body's beat
 matching movements.

For the sounds that seep into my skin.
Penetrating, piercing my eardrum drumming
 strumming my captivated collective.
Mentally lapping a language that's beyond linear
 linguistics.
Taking in all I can take, I assimilate the visual
 verbiage that's shaking my mind body soul.

I am a
>   house
>   music
>   junkie.

WHEN IT RAINS

In the summer around late June
Under a new moon.
I was stretched across my boudoir.
Soaking up the sweet smell of a rain breeze flowing
    through my window.

Earthy crisp wet wind.
Drip drop rain on my window pane clashed softly
    at a steady growing pace.
I rolled over for yet another taste.

Tap tap.

The rain and window fusion brought on some
    confusion.
Do my ears deceive me?

Tap tap.

I thought it was the rain tapping, but appears to be
    someone rapping.
To my surprise my eyes were not telling lies as I
    took in the vision before me.
His eyes were like thunder with a smile like
    lightning.
Strong yet gentle.
Soaking wet and sexy.

RAINY PAYNE

Umbrella is a good idea to forget.

"Come inside my dear, before you catch a cold."

"Why don't you come outside?"

Off my bed I rolled.

Mid summer's rain.
Warm, warm thunderstorm.
Cover me with your love and cleanse my heart and soul.
Wash away my troubles.
Wash away all my fears.
Wash away my pain.
As I dance with the man that only comes around when it rains.

An orchestra of a million drops played at our feet.
As we danced gliding sliding to a liquid melody.
Standing kneeling laying, my thoughts were swimming and saying,

Damn girl.
Have you slipped into
some crazy lucid dream?

I was too curious to scream.

Liquid lips lapped slapped clapped and cling.

LOVE SPELL

Licking.
    Dripping.
        Tripping on the thought.
    Soaked to the bone.
Wet free and on fire.

Bodies merged under sheets of showers.
I could feel him seeping through my clothes.
Under my skin as we touched and melted.
Entangled, entrapped in this connection.
Drunk from his wet intoxication.
Eyes closed in climax of this perfection.

Drop drip.

Relaxed and lost in his script.
I didn't realize my visitor was fading.
Shading off to a color of pale, pale blue.
My night was turning into a solo review.
The echo of thunder in the distance, the shimmer of
    lightning from afar.
No farewell or good night.
When I open my eyes to nothing in sight nor
    sound.
Other than water trickling into a drain.
I stand alone thinking of the man I will see again
    next time it rains.

RAINY PAYNE

PLAY

You have the dance floor under your control with
 your fingertips.
Finding the groove of my vinyl skin my soulful
 riffs revolve; as you tap into my melody.
Cross fading what chaos created into control,
 seamlessly putting me in a trance.

I find myself lost.

My eyes closed so I can feel every layer.
As the high-five frequency weaves in and out of
 me.
Changing my chemistry.
Bouncing between my vertebrae shaking my
 senses.
My hips swing and sway to the recorded rhythm.
Sweat drippin'.
I listen with every pore.

Last night a DJ saved my soul.

Your delicious vibes got me floating and lost in this
 house… music.
Hit me like a drug and I am trippin', as a DJ is
 rippin' up the decks bringing me home.
My only addiction, the DJ, is the doctor filling my
prescription of mad flavor.

Getting my nightly dose in the middle of this ambiance.
Keeping score.
Slipping, sliding, gliding, fiending for more.

Lost in this mix master's harmonic paradigm.
I find sanctuary on the dance floor where I become sound.
Turning me on.
Taking me higher.

I get tingling sensations with every vibration.
Spinnin' beat blendin'.
You give me what my body needs and my soul desires.
Playing me over and over and over and over again and I love how you turn me out.
Because deep inside, my heart beat matches the drums pumping, thumping, pounding.
Sounding like an exquisite symphony to my once fragmented consciousness.
But your sensual sounds surround my senses.
Bringing me back home sweet house music.

ERASE

A choice on my path I made with caution.
But I still carelessly fell into your arms.
Your smile.
Your light.
It's because your focus slowly freed my infatuation.

More like my frustrations.

I let my heart and soul go for that second as you
    stepped out of my dreams and touched me.
But could you even feel?
Me played by you.
The one that got away.
You wiggled astray and slowly slip through my
    fingers like sand and water.
Dissolving my dreams.
Now like a melody, you me meander in my
    memories.
Still too fresh to face.
Unfortunate, I have to retrace you to erase…
You were everything to me, not knowing I meant
    nothing to…

You were that breeze that brought me peace.
Knowing your calm would cool my heat.
Your kiss was my antiseptic.

Such a sweet sting.

Your eyes would make love to me from across the room.
Sending pulsations.
Vibrations.
A symphony would sound a sensual score as you played me.
Like a melancholy cello with my soul strings sliding under your fingers.
Twisting tweaking my thoughts.
Where we lovers or friends?
Or maybe you thought I was a pro.
Though you never paid me.
You just played me.

The sound of your voice still bellows, echoes, lingers in the air.
And I dare go back to how we were.
I dare hold on to the new love that you let go.
Losing my grace as I try to erase you from my thoughts.
So, I try not to think.
But the poetry we wrote was in ink.

Please, someone give me something to ease my pain.
Cause just hearing your name puts a strain on my… intellect.
I've tried not to concentrate on your confusion that has somewhat crippled my creativity.

LOVE SPELL

Recalling the life I had before where there was so much serenity.

Though I kept falling, you were not there to catch me.
My heart weakened in your wake and I crashed.
I've tried to pick up the fragments.
With each piece reclaimed I realize more and more, I was nothing but a game.

I would love to hate you.
But you still control my actions.
Because when we would embrace, I never thought I would be replaced.
You plan this perfect escape.
Not so much a chase, but just for me to be running in place.
How can something so strong be so easily erased?

I must confide in my pride that's been pushed aside and make peace with my passions.
Finding another focus.
Should be easy?
Right?

RAINY PAYNE

TO MY SONG

You are my love song.
Your kiss is a lyrical serenade.
Your touch a melody.
With one solitary glance my will bends like musical reverberations.
Intonations echoing your auric vibrations.
Softly striking harmonic cords.
Directing the pace of my sense's symphony.
Redefining what music means to me.

Rest, one, two.

Blushing, rushing, overheating.
My heart drumming beating tones that are tuned to the resonance of our tender revelry.
Enveloped in an intoxicating articulation.
A ballad your body sings to mine.
I track your confident cadence as you take your time.
Marinating in melodious sensuality.

Rest, one, two, three.

When we come together, our dissonance transposes to a counterpoint of grace.
An aria with notes arranged in unity.
Each movement uttered in perfect key with

overtones worthy of ovation.

I can't keep still.
Still listening to the silence of your sighs over and
    again is akin to an adagio of dramatic refrains.
My inner arrangement rumbles and rattles hitting
    hertz heard only at high octave range.
Our frequencies meet at equal tempos, mental,
    emotional, and physical.
I chime to your fingers like the strings of a violin.
My lover, my song, my friend.

Rest, one, two, three.

THE WAITING GAME

Once upon a time.
In a land not so far away.
Lived a little lady playing the waiting game.
Now, I know this story may sound the same as all
 those tall tales told trying to teach about true
 love.
Leaving gullible little girls with the goal to hold
 onto.
With hope that someday her prince would come.
Waiting for that day when a handsome man would
 prevail and break some sorcery's spell.
Then presto, all her problems will dissolve with
 just one kiss.
And she won't have to turn back into a pumpkin
 or fish.
But I think there's been something I've missed.
Cause in my experience he doesn't exist.

All I ever wanted was someone who would meet
 me halfway up that castle wall.
Someone who would be willing to get that glass
 slipper altered to fit.
Some very special guy who would look into my
 eyes and see love locked inside; and want to
 claim that as his prize.
But I've only been a magnet for men that sweep me
 off my feet.

Then ten minutes later fall asleep.
Leaving me frustrated and faithless from all those fairytales and magic spells that; led me to believe there was a prince waiting for me.

I am seduced into their web with poison promises posing as perfumed poetry.
Mixed with magical mendacity.
They check in, to quickly check out.
Leaving behind loosened layers of me that fall like the petals of an enchanted rose.
As the frog turns into a toad.
And the beast is still a beast.
You see.
In the end; the clock, wine, sweet songs, and candlelight all lied to me.

Life is no fairytale.
Like the dreams that live between the countless shelves of storybooks that fill the nooks of my childhood memories.
Instead of the perfect mate fate sends me knaves with cracks in their crown.
And each hit of heart ache makes it harder to heal and tell apart the fake from the real.
Molding my high standard stigma that's been stitched together from pages of seemingly innocent childhood fantasies.
Before we have even met, the man is a legend of all time in my mind.
Shamefully so, I am always left alone to ask,

LOVE SPELL

"Where is my prince?"

Where is this man?
A knight in shining armor that's aimed at an ardent attempt to rescue and recovery his sleeping beauty that's been bewitched by blind faith?
Where is my definition of true love?
The lyric to my melody manifested from middle age manuscripts.
A marksman who will target my heart and teach me what true love is meant to be.
My sweet reprise.
Who will catch my tears before they reach my eyes.
A noble chivalrous champion; that will color my world with unconditional compassion and patiently put each piece back in place.
The one that carries the key to the fairytale I refuse to forget.
Because I'll still continue to compare.
With starry eyes, searching for my crystal castle in the air.

Though it's full of fallacy and regret.
I hope that one day he and I will get.
To walk hand in hand into the sunset.
And live happily. Ever. After.

RAINY PAYNE

AMNESIA

In one hand I hold the future.
The other embraces the past.
Forgotten and unknown though I am shown
    scattered scribbled scripts on fading pages.
Loose leaves that linger in the dense fog.
The haze in my head.
Of what I have done and said.
Because I've lost half my life, time, and memories.

Just thinking makes me quiver when tempted to
    remember who I really am.
How I came to be, to feel, to see.
To draw this breath on the edge of a dream that
    doesn't end.
I begin to resort to faith, but I've forgotten what it
    means.
Shame how I've fallen and take the blame.

I feel like a failure.
Pushing me farther from what I was.
My existence is empty and isolated.
Where the vague seems vivid.
Consumed in a room filled with vacant flashbacks
    that haunt me.
I would cry, but I know I won't remember.
Why try to put a puzzle together when the pieces
    just don't fit?

What was once photographic is now stitched
    together by shredded bits of string.
Stretch across inter-dimensional fragments of time.
Carefully encapsulated in the deep recesses of my
    mind.
In one hand I hold the future and the other
    embraces the past.
    The beginning and the end.
Never to be retrieved again.

LO.V.E

Love is a sickness and I seem to be immune.
All the talk of its tenderness is a bit too touchy for me.
Or maybe because the baggage I have is a bit too heavy for it to hold.
As much as I would like to lounge in its loveseat made for two, I must pass.
But I'd like to dissect the word, to awaken the weary of what we're up against.
Before we begin, to let L-O-V-E wander into our heart space again.

L is for the layers of emotional latency leaving invisible lesions that linger for life.
Living like you lucked out on the love lottery.
It liberally lubricates your libido and learning.
Going deeper and deeper into loves uplifting light.
Or feeling locked in a lonely lull with heavy luggage you latched onto at low price.
The lips that used to leave you lightheaded and lustful, now only lecture about the liability to your lineage.
Leverage so you won't leave.

O is for the obscure object one seems to obsess over at every opportunity.
Optimistically open to obtain organically or

otherwise.
The opiate you are on after an overdose of emotions.
O is for not wanting to be ostracized for being only one from the outspoken society we occupy.
Who made the outline, and why should I comply?
Over rule, override... nuff said.
There will be less overhead.

V is for vanity when love is gain for valor.
A vacant value valuable only to a vampire.
Leaving you a vexed victim.
V is for love a vocalist that speaks vivid volumes at low vibration.
In time a vine vintage or a vile vinegar.
Making a victor a victim to its various vices.

Listen, L.O.V.E.
You can't make me tipsy on your luxurious liquor that makes one lose their reliability.
I know the low games you play, you see.
That's why cupid's arrow keeps missing me.

E is for how easy one can involve the ego to elaborate on what love should feel like, look like.
Complete with encouraged ideas of emasculation if emotions are openly expressed and emptiness if embraced to eagerly.
The epidemic of love shows side effects too subtle to see.

E is the enigma etched in my mind that only entertains my thoughts.
Ever evaluating what it means to be an expressive expression of.
After everything has ended and can evaluate the evidence, eventually realize the extreme error you were put through.
L.O.V.E. has some explaining to do.

L.O.V.E.

L... O... V... E.

RAINY PAYNE

ON A DAY LIKE THIS

Umbrella is a good idea to forget is what I say, on a day like this.
On a day when puddles become pools under your feet.
This rainy day.
This liquid street.
Drip drops falling on my head that's swimming with memories of your smile.
That smile is a sunbeam on this cloudy day.
The light that shines the way.
As the rain is falling and calling my name, I get drenched in what feels like love.
Soaking all my senses, this shower is a serene serum as I make my way.
Would you follow my soft slippery stroll marked by a melody?

Ba, ba, ba, babaaa. ba ba ba da da ba.
Ba, ba, ba, babaaa. ba ba ba da da ba.

With no particular pace and place to go.
I flow,
      I slide,
           I dip,
                  in this precipitation.

My heart skips a beat in the swell of anticipation of

seeing you again.
When we can chat about the weather.
We can talk about whatever.
When I can lose myself in your eyes, like I've lost
 myself in this lighthearted linger.
This storm sounds like a soft spoken soggy
 symphony.
Bewitching as the rain bathes me in beautiful
 benevolence.
Soaking my sodden clothes clinging to me.
I should seek some sort of shelter, but the thunder
 rumbles my restless reasoning.
And with each wet step the rain sings to me.

Ba, ba, ba, babaaa. ba ba ba da da ba.
Ba, ba, ba, babaaa. ba ba ba da da ba.

Maybe I am mad.
Senseless is what one would say.
To mark my heart with raindrops that would only
 fade away.
This is no riddle, no game, and after today I will
 remain the same.
The same woman that is in love with you… in love
 with the rain.
When I show up at your doorstep, my heart is what
 I bring.
On a day like this when I sing.

    Ba, ba, ba, babaaa. ba ba ba da da ba.
    Ba, ba, ba, babaaa. ba ba ba da da ba.

CLOUDS

Sweet summer rain speaks to me in quatrains and
 sonnets.
Scattered within rhythmic pitter patter.
Putting a sodden spell on a normally noiseless
 night.
I know the sky is covered in a gray shaded shroud
 as lightning plays games with the clouds.
The thunder's hollow roll roused me from sleep.
Deep in dream from the earlier hours' sorcery you
 weaved in me.

I feel the weight of your arm weekly wrapped
 around my waist.
Our legs in a delicate embrace as if you don't want
 to chase me in slumber.
Your breath gives a soft caress to my nape and I
 think how I hardly want to escape this moment.
This feeling of you with me.
On a night where the roll of thunder isn't the only
 thing that shakes the foundation, rattles the
 walls, loosens my senses.

A sublime subtle breeze caresses the smell of the
 wet night air.
It's like a cool knife that cuts through the warm
 steam of this dream realized in a dark room.
Where the passionate air dares to play games with

the shadows.
They seem to shine as they dance to the sound of the summer's serenade.

Slowly, my eyes open just as lightning freeze frames your face.
Your honey eyes glow as though I am a long-lost lover finally found from eons ago.
I happily hand over my heart one blissful blink at a time.
With your eyes locked on mine.
Speechless in the sumptuous silence that touches, traces transparent tethers that held my composure together.

Our love is beyond what is verbalized.
We're in a marriage of mind, body, and soul.
Vocalized through vibration.
Hearing on a heart level.
The softest shade of loud.
And I know the sky is covered in a gray shaded shroud as lightning plays games with the clouds.

NIGHT VISION

Breaking my home bound bondage with the buzz
> by no means of some cheap thrill.

I head out on a midnight excursion.
Crusin'.
Moving amongst strangers.
I smoothly slip into the rhythm of the night.
Might be the full moon magic that's stirring my
> steps.

Cause my jeans can't keep up with my hips... can't
> keep pace with my feet.

I stride riding the gain of my body's beat, as I night
> sight see the city streets.

The summer steamy steam is oh so thick.
With a click, click of my heels tap tapping on the
> concrete.

> *The sidewalk is teeming with traffic that's looking for*
> *trouble.*

I put my night vision on, and all my muddled
> misty mind turns to crystal, crystal clear.

My sense of sight turns to ultraviolet light vision.
Night vision.
My sensory perception is sensitive to the sounds
> that surround as I saunter.

Sucked into the saturation of this nocturnal
> atmosphere.

I...
Disappear deep into the delusion of this pre-dawn dimension.
Weaving in and wondering out.
My mind sheds fear with each step I steer closer to my destination.
Without too much hesitation, I enter.
My entire being instantly bonds with everybody bouncing, boogieing in this house.
Where love levitates the believers.
The bass seductively summons my soul to break it down...
     down,
          down.
Breathing new life into my body.
Taking me higher and my desires.
Wrapped up tight with my night vision.
Reveling in this repetitious rhythm.

Creating yet another chronicle in my consciousness.
Just like heaven house music heals a heavy heart.
Attack with each tasty track my man is spinnin'.
Giving me chills and thrills with no frills.
And I...
Can barely comprehend as a DJ is working me over.
It's his one and only mission with me wishing this would never end.
I close my eyes and with surprised I still have my

LOVE SPELL

night vision in place and I sweetly escape my
three dimensional prison.
Free falling floating in this flawless feeling.
Touched by the treble and it's becoming personal.

Perfecting my groove.
I am moved by this moment that is manipulating
me in more than words.
In more than sounds that are saturating my sweat
soaked skin.
I can't control what's happening with in me.
Deliriously dancing.
Keeping me on the edge of my feet.

I can't pretend.
I'm in a trance.
Hypnotize by the house music.
Resonating.
Penetrating.
I am sinking deep into the groove that has
internally changed me.
Rapidly rearrange my thoughts.
What it means to be, to see.
With my night vision on I am going strong into the
after-hours.

Though I know I'm not alone in the zone, I am
blown away by the beauty of beholds.
It's taking complete control.
Moving at high velocities.
Gliding like liquid free-flowing lucidity.

RAINY PAYNE

I try to make a mind-body connection for
 collection.
But the melodies grab me all over again, and again,
 and again.

LOVE DEFINED

Never thought I'd be the one to walk in this direction.
Facing so much affection that is just a reflection of where I stand.
Never thought I would be whispering words that would define the outline of my future life.
Love was a word reserved for that materialistic mask behind my broken dreams.
Or left unspoken for the one that wasn't... So it seems.
Words, words, words.
There are millions of books filled with billions of them at a time, but none so refine to define what you mean to me.
How I see you and me.
You relit the spark, a light I thought I lost long ago.
My heart had a hole hollowed from past mistakes of love.
In the meaning of...?
Confusing the cause.
Lessons gained, and it's hard to explain in words how you have opened me to feel.
I now know the word needs to be redefined from this day on.
Cause when I look into your eyes your soul speaks volumes alone.
So, can you be my definition of?

Cause you define love.

Looking up the word that everyone speaks of, dreams of.
Love, such a shallow syllable and shame to say for feelings sake.
Cause the language you awaken in my heart seems limited to a word that sounds so plain.
When I try to explain that your love has got me so high.
I don't know if I ever want to get over your ways that swayed me.
That gave me inspiration to create a world made for two.
You are the sound to my rhythm to my soul, shadowed in beauty.
Drenched in delicate decadent subtle notes known only in the finest wine.
Delivering a delicious dose of the meaning of daily.
You have blessed me beyond what my imagination can expand upon.
I am humbled to have you in my life.
Every day I thank the creator of creators for sending me the true definition.
Because simply by being who you are, you define love.

PEN, PAPER, PROSE

I bleed black blood on blank notes reciting quotes
 from my heart.
It starts when I pick up pen, my emotions begin to
 give in to what wells within.
Like the ink I sink in the script that drips and flows
 from a formless foundation.
Unfolding words between sheets of paper;
 scribbled quips that snip seams from a
 subconscious unconscious mind.

I am a magnetic pole, shifting through thoughts
 that translate from my fingertips and glossed
 lips that kiss memories of past life parallels.
My prose unfolds like a rose exposed to the sun.
Whispering its soft scent of words that hang like
 clouds in the rain.
I am a creator of creation.
Movement in motion.
Of bone and flesh.
A divine deviant dreamer, feeler, thinker.
Filling in the gaps between two generations of
 conformity.
Comfortably cushioned in the cradle of the
 creator's limitless outline.
I define the richness of a creative soul through
 which all has arose.
I am pen, paper, prose.

RAINY PAYNE

LESS THAN

If you were to put me on a scale, would I weigh
    less in your mind?
If you find my physical not appealing revealing,
    am I invisible?
Though I glow, would you not bestow your
    attention?
Would another eclipse the light you don't see in
    me?
Would I be less than a woman?

Would I be a disappointment when my body has
    aged after we have engaged in conception?
Not looking like my finest hour.
Would you care?
Or would you send me packing for what you think
    I'm lacking?
In your eyes would I be less than a woman?
    If I were a stay at home or worked my will and
    body to the bone creating a comfortable home;
    would your love be less shown?
Would you conspired to retire me?
Would you think me unworthy?
Would you leave me to wonder why you stopped
    trying to attain and contain the flame that is my
    inner fire?
That is being a woman.

Would you need me?
Would you want me?
Would you attest to the unrest my soul imposes as
    I independently draw out your insecurities?
Challenging your sensitive masculinity.
You understand, as a man, my love is so deep.
You might drown just at the thought of being held
    in my cocoon, my womb.

If my words speak my heart speak my mind,
    would you find me less than your respect?
Or, would you try to protect the *weaker* sex?
Would you prefer me seen not heard?
Just a vision?
A bird?
A star?
A car?
Or anything less than a woman?

When you try to damage my dignity by habitually
    hitting me.
Trying to breach what you cannot reach.
What's woven in my intricate womanly tapestry.
Trying to break me down to your level with your
    domination.
Did you forget that I'm creation?
When you see the scars beneath, would you stay?
Or would you take your last breath and walk
    away?
Justified in judging me while you are judging
    yourself, really.

LOVE SPELL

Knowing you are... less than a woman.

RAINY PAYNE

CONNECTED

In the moment.
Just making movement with my breath.
Taking to the throne of my divinity.
Falling fathoms from with inside out-ward-ly
    projecting.
Leaving behind this simple shell you see.
In search of the unseen source, the unknown me.
Relaxed and ready for whatever is shown.
Phasing out of the physical fear, fatigue, fault and
    focus on leveling with love.
I resign to align my mind to the universe behind
    my closed eyes.
Merging with my maker.
All that is.
Drenched in the light despite myself.
My soul soaks in the soothing sounds of the
    stillness around my mind's eye.
I see all is connected to you, connected to me.

I am the spirit personified.
Perfect in every infinite possible way.
Divine.
Drifting in a sublime dream like state of mind.
I solicit a soul's sojourn.
Giving up guilt for gaiety.
I go deeper and deeper.
Expanding with each exhalation.

Filling my lungs with life.

Watching what works its way into my thoughts
 and letting it go.
Comfortably content with shedding the shame and
 blame.
This meditation is medicine.
Healing the holes in my heart.
Keeping me intrigued in this infinite moment to a
 vibration that internally growing groove in
 solitude.
Continuing to see life in its true form.
The connection to me.
The connection to you.

FLOWERS

Rising on the horizon.
Crossing untouched paths.
We follow the wandering souls that make nothing out of nothing.
Constantly turning and twisting the caverns of your heart that beats to a drowsy melody.
Come dance with me and play your sweet song of life that flows through your veins.
We danced like petals adrift currents.
Swaying gently in and out over ripples.
Oh, and how they cry when found amongst smooth rocks on shore.
Clinging to hopeless inevitable peril in the sun; that bakes the memories of their dreams.
They flew and floated like angels through heaven with clouds lifting up their hearts.
"It's over." They cry. "The dance is over and we have not yet gotten our feet soaked in the liquid of a long forgotten paradise."
Oh, how can this be?
Because the river flows from miles.
Spraying its richness through the winding valley.
Reflecting its goodness for all to see.
Traveling through denseness of thick fractions of a second concentrated into the mountain.

RAINY PAYNE

TWO YEARS

Should have known better than to play the game.
Could've done better is what they were all saying.
Would've known better, but my heart now has a
    hole where your so called love used to live.
I should have seen the signs.
Read between the same weak lines that the
    previous relationship wreck worked on me.
Instead, I fled right back into my pitiful pattern that
    pretends to be protection.
So, I swallowed your pill and now feel as small as a
    single grain of sand; in the palm of your hand.
As my misery expands at your command.
Aware of the world around, but I could only be
    found on an island of isolation.
Incarcerated for the crimes of my devotion.

I thought love could cure anything, so I stayed and
    paid with my body.
My mental state that you stripped down to deep
despair.
While you'd continuously compared me, I would
    consign my comfort for conformity.
As you constantly cut me into little bits of shit that
    never really fit into your life.
Creating cracks and confirming that my self-esteem
    was a joke.
My love was held in place by words I wanted to

say.
Actions I wanted to make, but feared freedom from your heavy heart and hands.
For two years I was your personal paranoid paramour.
The one who was wholly lost in your lackluster love.
Content with your crafty crass.

Powerless.

Praying for your piety, but the only thing you did religiously was fucked me.
Literally.
Someone once told me to follow my heart, for it would never lead me astray.
Dare I say they have never been a predator's prey.
My heart and mind needed to have a direct line about what I thought all was fine.
But it just got worse.
You continued to hurt me every time.
If I would have known better, I would never have smiled at first flirt.
Never had that first kiss.
A kinky knife twist that kindled that untamed fire behind your eyes.
That flame that drained me of everything.
It has been years since I've escaped the nightmare, but nightly I struggle in my sleep.
I am subconsciously still trapped in the two years of torture.

LOVE SPELL

My methodical manipulator.
The devil that dwells next door.
The man who despite my devotion… My love
    could not fix.
I feel like fate has made some flaw in my fabric.
I would love to assassinate the assassin of a broken
    woman's heart; to heal the holes from the two
    years you stole.

But,…

Could of.

Would of.

Should of.

But I won't.

RAINY PAYNE

BEHIND CLOSED DOORS

When the doors close, I am down to drown in the
    steam from the warm stream between my
    thighs.
As we gently collide.
I'm not in business to play games.
The same as some strangers to this space.
Our one night love embrace traced back to where
    you called me, the manifestation of beauty.
Where you touched my hand on my knee and deep
    inside came a little scream.
A little dream.
Because I knew what was the score; when you
    would take me behind closed doors.

Some people say good things come to those who
    are willing to wait.
Reveling in a limbo state of anticipation.
Temptation.
We telepathically touch as you slowly undress my
    body.
Passion resides behind your eyes.
I am your prize.
Licking lips that say they need me, they want me.
It's hard to be oblivious to this obvious attraction
    between you and me.
What's going on and what's in store.
As I wait for you to take me from behind closed

doors.

Seems so natural how we both slipped between the sheets; they keep the secret spell you used to seduce me.

Because the moment we met, all I wanted was you inside my fantasy.

I'd be blind, fooling myself to pretend we'd be friends.

That there would be more pass this one magical night.

It's just best to ride these waves and enjoy each moment as they come... on the bed... against the wall, on the floor...

Behind closed doors.

PSYCHO

Per your request, I've written down a word or two
    for you.
The one that took my love as trivial.
The one that tricked a trophy to be a trinket that
    you tried to break beyond repair.
Dare I say your name?
Though you know who you are.
So… Maybe I'll just call you psycho.

Now, my intention is not to poke at your
    imperfections.
We all have our moments, our faults.
But for you, falling in love meant you failed fear.
A foe your ego friended years ago.
So, trying to teach you about my tenderness was
    like retraining a trollop to resist temptation.
Like training a troll for a triathlon.
And the tiniest whisper of your weakness
    awakened a wrath where the punishment
    didn't match the crime.
Making such a scene made for the silver screen.
The evidence was evident every day.
When I'd wake wondering what emotional high
    low high you would be wading in.

Now, I know you're not here to defend whatever
    you so needed to defend.

In the process, perplexing me with your explosive
   emotional episodes that elude even my intense
   imagination for expression.
You always seemed to get some satisfaction in
   completely confusing me with your off kilter
   convoluted conversations.

The F word follow the L.
The L would follow F.

After two months of this bullshit there was nothing
   of me left to give a pill popper, insane driving,
   chain-smoking, compulsive lying, unstable,
   angry, paranoid, purposely pushing all my
   freaking buttons at once individual such as
   yourself.

*Every time you raised your voice to shout, a louder voice
   inside of me said, "Get out."*

I had nothing left to lose when I gladly walked…
   No ran away from your arena, your game.
I've step to the side of your selfish sharp remarks
   that seemed a bit off note.
I now know you were out of your freaking mind
   psycho.

Yes, this goes out to you my dear.
With hopes that next time you will steer clear of a
   woman, I must say, that is just too much for
   you, anyway.

LOVE SPELL

I'd like to reclaim each monotonous moment meant
 to mend what we'd just begin.
Because in the end, we can't even remotely be
 friends.
So, please stop calling, texting, emailing, tweeting,
 and requesting to be my friend or my friend's
 friend.
Because this chase is only making you look more
 like a nutcase.
By a woman that has easily let you go.
And promised herself never ever again get
 involved with another psycho.

RAINY PAYNE

AFRAID

I am afraid that every time I turn the page it will be
    the same chapter.
Every time I read a line it will continue to define
    my future for the faults of the past.

I am not worthy.

I am afraid of turning each corner and being
    confronted by the cause of why it hurts to be in
    my skin.

I must stay silent.

I am afraid to fall asleep knowing no one wants to
    help me make the bed I've made.

So, I gave and gave and gave knowing like a slave I
    behaved.

No one loves me.

A shutter seems silent to the sensation shaking
    under my skin.

Nothing is simple.

Even when I rewind time in my mind to find your
    words still light in the air.

I must not hate myself.

RAINY PAYNE

I must not try to find a cause no, no, no, no… I must evolve, evolve, and evolve.

YOUR EYES

You have inspired.
Making a mental menagerie of this moment
    manifesting before me; I indulge in your
    delicacies.
Your eyes speak to me in telepathy as they tell me
    the truth of our destiny.

Luring me in.
Caught in the rapture of their stellar glow and
    trapped under your cool cascade.
I get chills, just close enough to fill the heat on your
    breath.

I slipped and fell, still falling, deeper and deeper
    into your stare.
I am not afraid to drown.
Your eyes make love to me as your focus slowly
    frees my infatuation.
Gets me high as my feet feel like feathers.
Cozy like a kiss and I am set adrift on the sea of a
    million shades of blue that warm and quiet my
    heart.
Beating breaking down my boundaries.
Beckoning me to rearrange my life for you.

Easy on my eyes, you visually saved me.

And though you are at a distance, knowing you makes me reach for hire echelons of coexistence.
Filling my emptiness with your abysmal blue quiet storm.
Where sonnets are sensually spoken without sound.

Words cannot describe the dreams your eyes draw me.
Painting perfect pictures.
Redefining the meaning of passion.
And if life is but a dream, I only wish to wake with you cuddled next to me.
So, the first thing I see upon the dawn of each new day are your eyes.

CARRY ON

Chill bumps rise like undulating waves.
Breath stuttered staggered movements marked
    with motionless momentum.
Each layer of my being feasts on feelings so real
    though I'm unrealistically wrapped in a dream.
His voice sensually sings my name as though it
    were his soul's song.
Dare I open my eyes to witness what would be a
    wishful blissful fantasy?
Or, do I allow this melody maker, this sweet gentle
    indulgent taker, to carry on?

RAINY PAYNE

UNSPOKEN

What's the use of spoken words with words that
 are left unspoken?
Words that leave my lips with a breath.
A kiss silences our synchronicity as we fearlessly
 fall into forever.
I knew the world would wait for this love.
For two to find they are one.
As you hold me unconditionally.
Where love is made with no movement.

In this space for sensual sensitive silence; you
 unwrap my delicacies deliciously.
My body a canvas where you paint love on my
 tapestry.
Slowly unbinding my inhibitions.
You make love easy.
Like breathing in the sweet perfume of our
 chemistry.
Before, I lost my way with love's clichés.
Judging my future from my past.

Love was lost to me.
Tucked away like an old memory.
Causing cautious confusion.
I felt my heart could break no more.
Then you stepped out of my dreams and touch me.

Settling my instability.
Solidifying my security in this surreal sequence of circumstance.
Mesmerized by this moment that separates us know more.

Before you love was like a shore without sand.
Like the sun without the feeling of warm.
Bass without a melody.
I am hypnotized by your humility; as you hold my heart with the heat behind your eyes.
Lavishing your love like a luxurious liquid that leaves me drunk with devotion.
Wanting more.

These words I dedicate to my love.
The man that has profoundly penetrated my protection.
My beautiful friend.
The one I keep within.
I will never stray.
What more to say, but I love you.
I love you.
I love you.

FREE SPIRIT

Tame is nothing to a free spirit that stays the same
 throughout time.
She travels the earth flowing with her friend the
 wind that picked her up at birth.
Carrying her to the far ends and back.
In her wake leaving lasting impressions and
 keeping pace never to slack.
She never settles and never glances back to the
 fading memory of what she was.
Yet she is always looking forward to the future at
 what she will be.
What she sees is her destiny of sojourning the earth
 like a bird.
Making her tracks invisible with only words.
Lyrics of her life in a place where she can't belong.
Because she can't stay too long to finish that eternal
 song of a free spirit.

Her steps trace the path that many already have
 taken, but for them now seems a path forsaken.
There is nothing transparent or fake about her ever-
 changing landscape.
Either in the mountains or on city streets; she is like
 a butterfly that spreads her wings to the sky
 and glides across the horizon.
Not stopping till she finds her prize and when will
 that be?

Making a tryst with time.

Free is the spirit that can make love with her mind and truly know she was created from all that is divine.
Free is the spirit that can breathe new life in every sigh in finds how deep her soul lies when she cries.
Free is the spirit that understands what you see is not who you really be... Free!

Spirit, continue to fly.
Make your eternal searching and wake the sleepers.
For a new day is coming where you find all you are seeking.
Tame is nothing to a free spirit that stays the same throughout time.
Searching for her eternal twin lover.
All the while the clock of life winds... On.

THE MEANS

I was here before, not noticing love was no more.
You said you wanted space, we were running in
    place.
The more I held onto you, the more it got tough.
I gave you a hundred miles, and it wasn't enough.
Now I stand alone.
Like I always am.
When will that be?
My chance to see the end of this dream.
The end of the means.

I was near before.
Not as distant as we've grown more.
My head is lost in this chase.
My body is missing your embrace.
The more I wanted you, the harder it became.
To let our love flourish.
It was a dying frame.
And now we stand in separate corners playing
    different games.

I must have been a fool to believe and be taken in
    by your inconsistency.
You say you love me one day.
Then the next you're not around.
All the time I am reaching for ground.
To submit to your torture.

RAINY PAYNE

To bow down at your request.
Must be a fool you have not yet second-guessed.

It seems.
I have to walk away from my first love.
Still searching, hoping to find the end to the means.

WHAT AM I?

Life is but a dream.
Donned in an opaque dressing gown.
Of silky soft spoken clowns that force feed fake
    desires.
Acting out scenarios of lies leaked from holes we
    have dug for ourselves.
To find ourselves somewhere within.
To make amends and begin again.

As we row, row, row, we feel the undertow of truth
    tugging.
But we do not slow the pace.
Because time is tick, tick ticking away toward the
    tomb that we feel we will fill tomorrow.
We exist in a world where skin defines the heart
    and mind.
The kind of world where the blind live like kings;
    and the meek are mocked for thinking outside
    of the mockery.
The hole, the grave of being a slave.
Being brave against a system that sucks your
    freedom of thought and speech by simply
    turning on a T.V.
Destroying the world while distracted with
    disposable homes, disposable clothes and cars,
    disposable integrity.
To take, take, take for the sake of convenience.

Completely content being controlled to the edge of unconsciousness.
Asleep and like sheep never asking.... What am I?

Am I the accuser or the accused?
The one that refused to let the light that lit the spark go dim.
Like a fragile fractal just barely holding onto this hyper hologram.
Am I just one of 7 billion sovereign souls that hold the key to release a life worthy of remembering?
Worth forgetting and starting over again.

Beginning at birth I was a blank page, impressed with heart in heaven.
Awake to awaken each day knowing my true nature is not to numb my connection to the one.
Where I come from.
Learning when I want to run.

Reality is just a another void filled with duality that lives and breathes.
Bites and screams.
Cuts and bleeds.
And we are the creator's conscious or un.
Believably following from fear.
Propaganda pushed in the vacancies.
Callously carved out by media mind control.
Posing as the perfect friend.
Convincing you of convoluted convenience.

LOVE SPELL

Separating you from self and everyone else.
While leaving you empty and lost to look for what this life really is about.

So, when you are finally free from mental constraints and you wake, what will you realize?
When you step up to see what a wasteland we have created around material judgment, what will you manifest?
Should be easy to bring into being.
When one walks with wide eyes the world will wake with you.
The truth has been translated out loud in all patterns and sounds present.
No passport or payment with plastic needed to know...

What am I?

RAINY PAYNE

REMEMBER ME

Remember me when I'm gone.
Will you remember my time with love in your
 heart?
With my smile on your mind.
Remember my kindness
My generous soul.
Recall the moment we met.
The first night you slept, knowing you would see
 me in your dreams.
We live for only a moment, so remember me.

Remember.
How I grew.
How my words took action.
Creating my mood.
Changing time.

Remember me and how the sun would rise in my
 eyes.
The moon would set on my skin.
How we became lovers and friends.
How time seemed so long, but was just a heartbeat.
An eye wink.
From now, remember me.

www.ingramcontent.com/pod-product-compliance
Lightning Source LLC
Chambersburg PA
CBHW022123040426
42450CB00006B/814